Introduced in 1934, complete and original boxed set of 28-series Vans. Original price 4/6. For further information see pages 49 to 51.

British Diecasts

A Collectors Guide to 'Toy' Cars, Vans & Trucks

G. M. K. Thompson

Also available from the Haynes Publishing Group –

'Scalextric – An Enthusiast's Guide' by Gillham (F286).
'Spot-On Diecast Models' – A Catalogue & Collector's Guide
by Thompson (F304).

ISBN 0 85429 264 0

© **G.M.K. Thompson 1980**

First published April 1980. Reprinted 1983

A FOULIS book

Published by
Haynes Publishing Group
Sparkford, Yeovil, Somerset BA22 7JJ, England

Distributed in North America by
Haynes Publications Inc
861 Lawrence Drive, Newbury Park, California 91320 USA

Editor **Rod Grainger**
Cover design **Phill Jennings**
Layout design **Lynne Blackburn**
Printed in England by J.H. Haynes & Co Ltd

6

Contents

Acknowledgements

The author wishes to express his sincere thanks and appreciation to all those involved with the production of this book. Particularly, Eric Morgan who generously allowed me access to his superb collection of 22-series Dinky models, to Roy Rousell with his collection of Spot-On and Corgi models and to Gill Carroll who spent many evenings typing the manuscript.

I must also mention my sincere gratitude to my wife, Janet, who was left alone at home during many evenings and weekends whilst I was working on this book.

Graham Thompson

Foreword

I first met Graham Thompson when I attended a film show on vintage buses held at the Pen Mill Hotel, Yeovil, Somerset, on one cold, miserable and wet November evening in 1975. I sat next to him, and during the course of conversation it was soon established that we both had a great interest in common – collecting diecast 'toys'. Within the next few days he visited my home to see my collection, and I his; we have been very close friends ever since.

Apart from his family life, and his work, Graham's priority in life is the history and collecting of diecast model vehicles. I would consider him to be one of the most knowledgeable collectors of diecast 'toy' models in this country today, but not only is he a keen collector he is also an excellent restorer of miniature vehicles as this book will prove. He has a natural gift for repairing early Dinky Toys which have suffered the usual complaint, metal fatigue, and he has the ability to blend paint to match with the original model colours. He does this for fellow collectors who are unable to get a similar 'toy' in 'mint' condition.

In conclusion I would add that this book is essential for all collectors of diecast models, not only to look back and say 'I had one of those toys when I was a child', which is so often said, but also for the serious collector who can look up details of a model in a few seconds without having to refer to various other pages in the book to find its origin and history.

I wish Graham and the publisher every success with this book and I sincerely hope there will be more to follow.

E. Morgan.

Eric Morgan
Yeovil, 1979

Introduction

My reasons for writing this book are a mixture of fond memories of childhood fantasies and an interest in the history of miniature diecast 'toy' vehicles that has stayed with me into adult life.

My intention is to explain by word and picture how the four main British diecast toy manufacturing companies and their products have progressed over the years and I have endeavoured to include as many of the really rare models as possible many of which feature uncommon colour variations. Also included are a few models from the French Meccano factory for the purpose of comparison. Although these particular French models were not originally sold in the UK they are obtainable in collecting circles.

The information supplied by this book is not intended to represent a complete cataloguing of every model produced by these four companies. I, therefore, make no apologies for omitting certain vehicles – everyone has their own favourites!

As you study my book you will observe the changes which have occurred from the early days of plain one-piece lead models to the high standard of today's designs with their opening doors, spring suspension, windows, etc; but, as with the full-size vehicles, will they survive the test of time?

Also detailed within these covers are the familiar boxes which were supplied with each model vehicle. Although most of these boxes were thrown away upon original purchase some have survived and if still in good condition add value and interest to the models they contain.

Any collectable diecast model is obviously worth more if in 'mint' condition and if it has its original box. The value of rare vehicles is greatly enhanced if they are in original condition; nevertheless, even if they have been mutilated or damaged in any way, it is definitely worthwhile to restore them. Inevitably, these rare models will become even scarcer in the future, so although a restored model will never have the same value as its 'mint' original counterpart it will still be a valuable asset to any collection.

To assist the serious collector, every model featured has been given a 'rarity value'. Because the value of these models moves ever upwards, almost on a daily basis, it was not practical to include actual monetary values; however, the information given should be sufficient to establish a *relative* value for most models.

The future of the diecast 'toy' is unknown, but at present collecting still flourishes, so I will complete my introduction by wishing you many enjoyable years of collecting these fascinating models.

**Graham Thompson
Yeovil, 1979**

Chapter One

A Collector's Guide

The best sources of old models in the UK are the swap meets held at various times of the year in venues as diverse as Gloucester, Bournemouth, Windsor and Yeovil. To find the exact time, date and location of swap meets the *Exchange & Mart* is a very useful guide (details being listed under the toy section). At these meetings the variety of models available for sale and exchange is almost endless.

If you are looking for a particular model at a swap meet the best practice is to check on the price asked, providing there are a few examples around, as this will vary from stall-to-stall and it is therefore easy to pay too much for a model.

Of course you must expect to pay more for a 'mint' example rather than a chipped or repainted one; it depends on what you are looking for. Spares are also available from stallholders, such as headlamps, tyres, radiators and steering wheels.

It is still possible to find old models in 'junk' shops and sometimes in antique shops; here the price may be a lot lower but watch out, as most people tend to think of all old models as being valuable even though, sadly, this is not the case and you could well find yourself paying too much.

Other sources are toy shops where it is possible, sometimes, to buy a model which has recently gone out of production, at the original list price, maybe even cheaper – it pays to shop around! Many model hobby shops nowadays sell (and buy) obsolete and collectable diecast models. Lastly most of the motoring and model hobby magazines and, of course, *Exchange and Mart*, feature 'ads' for these models among their classified advertisements.

Part of Eric Morgan's collection showing how an interesting and varied display of Models can look if properly laid out

How to store and display models

From the collector's point of view the best way of displaying models is the fitted glass cabinet with lighting, which is fine if you can afford it and have plenty of room. However, smaller glass cabinets can sometimes be purchased from 'junk' shops or other shops closing down, often very cheaply, depending on the size of your collection.

Another way of dealing with the problem is to obtain suitable wood and make up a few shelves; this is probably the cheapest way of displaying your collection providing you have time to dust your models frequently. Large collections tend to lose visual impact if models are placed too close to one another, so try to avoid this problem. Direct sunlight is another danger as, given time, this will cause paint to fade and metal to craze.

When planning a layout for your display area, try to arrange things so that models of different scale sizes do not clash.

Models which will be stored rather than displayed should, if they are not boxed, be wrapped carefully in tissues or foam sheting and be packed fairly tightly into larger but sturdy cardboard boxes (empty spirit bottle 'cases' are ideal). If you wish to store your models individually, proprietary cardboard boxes are available. Storing models may be difficult as a lot of pre-War models suffer from metal fatigue you must therefore keep them in an even temperature.

Construction

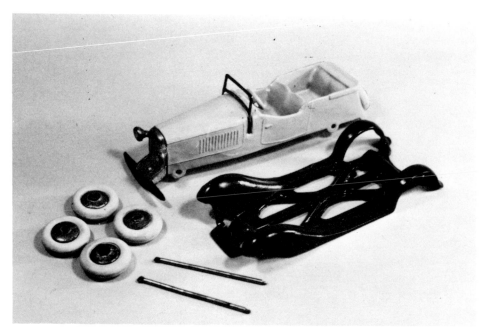

1) Dinky construction of the 1930s using the axles to hold the model together

2) Shown on the right, the one-piece casting used by Dinky in the 1930s, while the Citroen DS (on the left) displays the familiar tinplate base held on with rivets; a system adopted by Dinky, Corgi and Spot-On which is still being used

3) Lesney construction in which the bottom is riveted to the top

4) The standard system used by Dinky for their Supertoy range from 1947 until the late 1950s. The front tinplate base is clamped in, as are the rear axles; the load area slots into the cab at the front and the rear is held in by a long bolt and nut

5) For a time during the late 1960s and early 1970s the model was held together by two screws

6) A novel idea by Corgi in the late 1960s, whereby the fully-detailed chassis could be removed

Renovation

1) The project car Corgi Mini Marcos before restoration, showing several coats of paint which have been applied over the years and its generally very poor condition

2) 1st stage is to drill the rivet out.

3) The components which make up the model. Plastic interior trim can be cleaned with an old toothbrush soaked in soapy water. Windows sometimes can be polished to remove scratches using a mildly abrasive cleaner, such as metal polish

4) Stripping the body of layers of paint using proprietary paint stripper suitable for metal. Note that all plastic components must be removed before using this process

5) Polishing the bare body casting with fine steel wool

6) Spraying the body with a proprietary touch-up paint aerosol

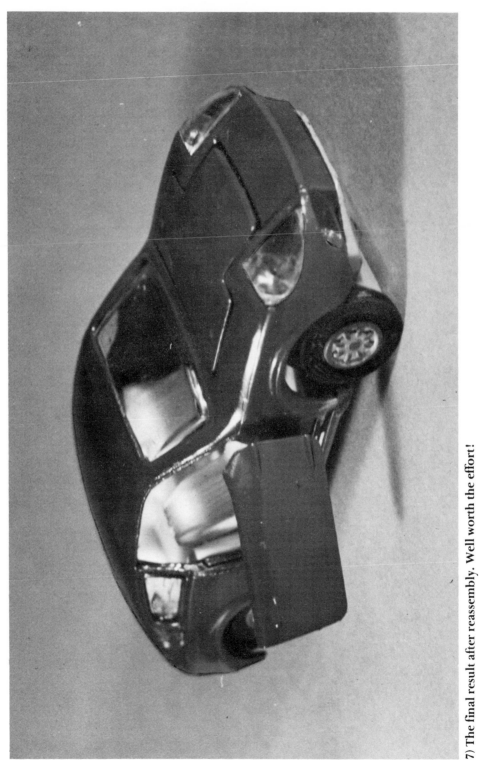

7) The final result after reassembly. Well worth the effort!

Chapter Two

Dinky Toys

Meccano, as a company, dates back to 1907 when Mr. Frank Hornby, a Liverpool man, took out a patent for his constructional toy made from metal parts which bolted together. He named his company after this toy, called 'Meccano.' Frank Hornby's company soon became world famous and later introduced 'O' gauge clockwork and 'O' gauge electric trains. In the late 1930s 'Dublo' gauge trains were manufactured and are still going strong today.

Model vehicles were first made available in December 1933 to add extra realism to model railways. The first vehicles were originally named 'Modelled Miniatures', though later in 1934 they became known as 'Dinky Toys.'

These very first models contained considerably more lead in the castings than subsequent models, which were manufactured of an alloy consisting of zinc, aluminium and magnesium known as Mazak or Zamak. This material, unfortunately accounts for metal fatigue in some of the earlier vehicles. The problem is caused by poor metal mixing resulting in instability over long periods of time – the metal bends and cracks and generally loses its integrity thus making the model very fragile.

The very first models were simple one-piece castings, with metal axles and wheels; they were available as a set of six in a box, or were sold separately for 6d each. Surprisingly none of these first models carried any headlamps.

Prices went up to 1s 3d due to the addition of purchase tax which was brought into operation in October 1940. New models continued to be introduced each month until the second World War when the company ceased to produce toys (sometime in 1941).

Dinky Toys were re-introduced in 1945 with models which were mostly produced before the War. One of the first new models to appear was number 38e The Armstrong Siddeley Hurricane. In 1947 a very successful line of heavy commercials known as 'Dinky Supertoys' was introduced; they were much larger than anything Meccano had previously offered, and were rather more expensive at 10/-. These larger, expensive models were largely bought as Christmas or birthday presents rather than everyday toys purchased by children with their pocket money. The boxes in which they were packed were plain and rather drab with a printed label describing the model. I believe boxes were not made available for cars and smaller models until 1953, when the smaller Dinky Toys came in small yellow cardboard containers with a coloured illustration on the sides and a model number on the end.

In 1956 with the arrival of 'Corgi Toys' Dinky obviously lost a share of the market. In 1958 they made up some lost ground with the introduction of plastic windows (available on Corgi right from the start) on a rather nice model of the A105 Austin Westminster. Fully sprung wheels came in 1959 with the Rolls-Royce Silver Wraith. I remember this model very well, as it appeared on television: the unique features, which included chrome-plated radiator and bumpers and working suspension, were fully described. (Price 5/6).

Towards the end of the 1950s, Meccano seemed to introduce more American cars than ever before; evidently these were aimed at the American Continent which was Dinky's largest export market.

Models with features such as opening doors and bonnet etc, appeared during the 1960s together with the rather poor 'Presomatic' steering.

Unfortunately 1964 proved to be the last year of Meccano as Lines Bros ('Triang' Manufacturers) took control of the firm in 1965. More recently the Airfix Group have taken control of Meccano following the collapse of Lines Bros.

With the introduction of one-piece plastic Speedwheels separate rubber tyres have been discontinued, which I think is rather a pity as although Speedwheels allow the model to run faster, they tend to spoil the general character of the vehicle. In most cases the traditional model boxes disappeared in favour of transparent plastic 'bubble' packs which displayed the model very well, but tended to break easily. Happily, there has been a recent reversion to the conventional box packaging with a transparent panel to display the model.

What of today? Well, certainly the range does not compare with that offered in Dinky's heyday, but while traditionalists may mourn, Dinky have to keep abreast of the times as evidenced by their new models which tend to be relatively cheaper and of poorer quality but follow 'space age' designs.

Rarity Value: Very rare

Introduction in 1934, Number 24c. Town Sedan finished in dark-blue with outside spare wheel and plated wheels, 1938-40 versions carried a radiator badge but no spare wheel. Both versions of this model are now virtually unobtainable. Original Price I/-

Introduced in 1934, Number 24d. Vogue Saloon with outside spare wheel; finished in light-blue and dark-blue. 1938-40 versions carried a radiator badge but no spare wheel. This model formed the basis of the later 36-series introduced in 1938 namely, 36c Humber Vogue. Original Price 9d

Rarity Value: Very rare

Rarity Value: Very rare

Introduced in 1934, Number 24e. Super Streamline Saloon; finished in red and maroon. 1938-40 versions carried a radiator badge, but to my knowledge were never fitted with a spare wheel. This model formed the basis of the later 36-series namely, 36d Rover Streamline. Original Price 9d

Introduced in 1934, Number 24f. Sportsman Coupe with outside spare wheel and plated wheels, finished in buff and brown. 1938-40 versions also carried a radiator badge but no spare wheel. This model also formed the basis of the later 36-series namely, 36b Bentley Coupe. Original Price 9d

Rarity Value: Very rare

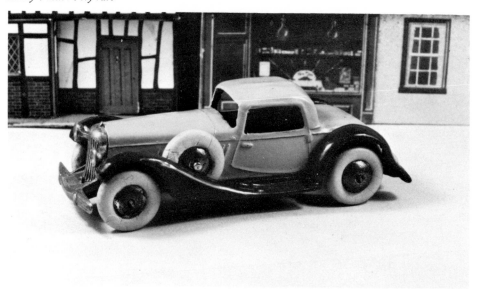

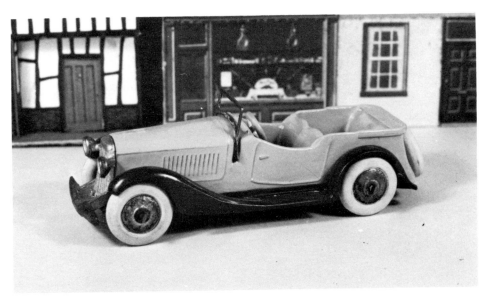

Rarity Value: Very rare

Introduced in 1934, Number 24g. 4-seater Tourer with open windscreen and rear-mounted spare wheel; finished in yellow and brown. 1938–40 versions were fitted with a solid windscreen and no rear-mounted rubber tyre. This model also formed the basis of the later 36-series namely, 36f Salmson 4-Seater Tourer. Original Price I/-

Introduced in 1934, Number 24h. 2-Seater Tourer with open windscreen and rear-mounted spare wheel; finished in yellow and black. This model was also modified as described for 24g; it also formed the basis of the later 36-series namely, 36e Salmson 2-Seater Tourer. Original Price I/;

Rarity Value: Very rare

Rarity Value: Very rare

Introduced in 1935, Number 30b. Rolls-Royce Saloon original pre-War shown with open chassis and white tyres; finished in grey and black. 1945-50 versions carried a plain chassis. Original Price 9d

Introduced in 1935, Number 30c. Daimler Saloon original pre-War shown; finished in Green and black. This model was also produced between 1945-50 in modified form as described for 30b. Original Price 9d

Rarity Value: Very rare

Rarity Value: Very rare

Introduced in 1935, No 30d. Vauxhall Saloon original pre-War with outside spare wheel and chequered radiator grille, finished in buff and brown. In the later versions of this car the chequered radiator and spare wheel were dropped; this version continued to be produced until 1948. Original Price 9d

Dinky Toys tinplate Filling and Service Station, introduced in June 1935, number 48 shown here with set Number 49 Petrol Pumps, introduced in June 1935. Original price of Service Station 1/6, Petrol Pump Set 1/6

Rarity Value: Fairly rare

Rarity Value: Rare

Dinky Toys tinplate Garage, introduced in December 1935, Number 45 with opening front doors to accommodate two Dinky cars. Original price 1/6

Introduced in 1935, Number 44. A.A. Set, Comprising 44a A.A. Hut, 44b A.A. Motor Cycle Patrol, 44c A.A. Guide (directing traffic), and 44d A.A. Guide (at the salute). Finished in yellow and black with tan figures. Original price of set 1/11. Shown in the foreground is Number 42b Police Motor Cycle Patrol and Number 37a Civilian Motor Cyclist

Rarity Value: Rare

Rarity Value: Fairly rare

Introduced in 1939, Number 38b. The Sunbeam-Talbot Sports, complete with steering wheel fitted in the dashboard and separate headlamp castings set into the wings. Example shown here finished in maroon with a grey tonneau-cover (note the transparent windscreen). Original Price 10d

Introduced in 1939, No 38d. Alvis 4-Seater Tourer fitted with steering wheel and transparent windscreen, this vehicle shows a certain charm in its design. Finished in maroon with grey interior. Original Price 10d

Rarity Value: Fairly rare

Number 38e. The Triumph Dolomite Sports never actually came onto the market although a prototype was produced together with a handful of samples for use in magazines and advertising. The car in this photo is my own conversion, made using No 40a Riley Saloon as the basis to show how the vehicle may have looked. The advertisement for the Triumph Dolomite was shown in June 1939 together with the other five cars in the set: the Frazer Nash, Sunbeam Talbot, Lagonda, Alvis and SS Jaguar of which three were marketed before production ceased in 1940. The Lagonda and Jaguar came out after the War, but for some reason the Dolomite was dropped to be replaced by the Armstrong Siddeley Hurricane, the first post-War car produced in 1946. Original Price 10d

Rarity Value: Fairly rare

Introduced in 1939, Number 39a. Packard Super 8 Sedan, a typical American car of the 1930s, very well detailed with the spare wheels cast into the wings. Finished in brown with black wheel hubs. Original Price 10d

Introduced in 1939, Number 39c. Lincoln Zephyr Coupe, a real 'classic' with its long flowing tail, built-in headlamps and 'waterfall' radiator grille. Finished in brown with black wheel hubs. Original Price 10d

Rarity Value: Fairly rare

Rarity Value: Fairly rare

Introduced in 1939, Number 39d. Buick Viceroy Sedan pre-War version; a super model for its time, featuring separate headlamp castings and moulded-in spare wheels. Finished in pale cream. Original price 10d.

Introduced in 1937, Number 34b. 'Royal Mail' Van pre-War shown with open rear windows finished in Red and black. This model was re-introduced after the War in a slightly different form with the rear windows filled-in and was produced until 1952. Original Price 10d

Rarity Value: Fairly rare

Rarity Value: Fairly rare

Introduced in 1937, Number 36g. Austin Taxi with driver, pre-War with open rear window, finished in blue and back. This model was also re-introduced after the war with the rear window filled in and was produced until 1949. Original Price 11d

Introduced in April 1946, Number 153. The Willys Jeep; a very well detailed model which is finished in olive drab with a white star on the bonnet, typical US Army colours. Original Price 2/6

Rarity Value: Fairly rare

Rarity Value: Fairly rare

Introduced in December 1946, Number 38E. The Armstrong Siddeley Hurricane Convertible was the first post-War car to be modelled. Finished in red with maroon interior, black steering wheel and a plastic windscreen; this car has a neat appearance but for some reason carried no door lines in the casting. Original Price 2/6

Introduced in July 1947, Number 40a. Riley 1.5-Litre features typical English styling with separate wings and running boards; headlamps are individual castings set into the wings. The version shown here is an early one finished in navy-blue with black wheel hubs; the baseplate carried small printing; later models carry larger printing. Original Price 2/6

Rarity Value: Easily obtained

Rarity Value: Fairly rare

Introduced in October 1947, Number 501. The Foden 8-Wheel High-Sided Truck. This was the first of a new line called Dinky Supertoys; they were much larger than anything Meccano had previously offered and were quite expensive at 10/-. This was the first of the many Fodens Meccano have produced; it differs from the second type in respect of the cab which is more rounded and the radiator is standard Foden type with the name clearly standing out

Introduced in October 1947, Number 513. Guy Flat Truck with tailboard; the version shown here is an early model which has early wheel hubs, straight-sided number plate fixing and the back axle is held in with two tinplate clips. On later versions the axle mounting was cast-in, the wheel hubs were changed and the number plate mounting was altered to have tapering sides. The bodywork is a good clean casting with the name Guy prominent on the radiator. Finished in yellow with a black chassis. Original Price 7/-

Rarity Value: Easily obtained

Rarity Value: easily obtained

Introduced in March 1948, Number 25M. The Bedford End Tipper being a firm favourite with children was a model which was produced for a long time. The tipping action and opening of the tailboard is achieved by a simple worm system which operates when turning a crank on the side of the chassis. Original Price 5/9

Introduced in October 1948, Number 25V. The Bedford Refuse Wagon, finished in fawn with green doors, has been fitted with the same tipping action as the Bedford End Tipper, number 25M, but with additional sliding tinplate covers and rear door. This popular toy has often been found amongst various Dinky collections and has been very popular with children in the past. Original Price 5/6

Rarity Value: Easily obtained

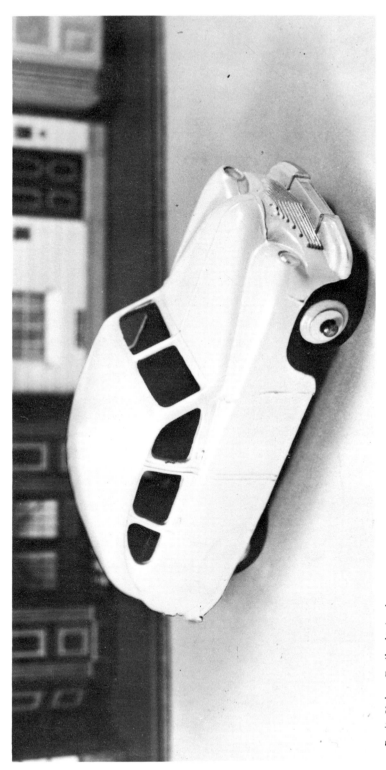

Rarity Value: Easily obtained

Introduced in November 1948, Number 40e. The Standard Vanguard again a very accurate model. There were three versions produced by Dinky. The first version, finished in fawn, had small print on the baseplate, the back axle was held in with a clip and bodywork did not feature spats over the rear wheels. The second version did have wheel spats, and the third version, finished in pale cream, had wheel spats, larger print on the baseplate and for some reason carried an extra moulding line on the boot lid which tended to spoil the appearance. This model was numbered 153 in 1955. Original Price 1/9, later versions 2/2

Rarity Value: Fairly rare

Introduced in December 1948, Number 504. The Foden 8-wheeled 14-ton Tanker was the first of the 8-wheeled tankers, again with the type I Foden cab. The tank which is tinplate, formed the basis of the later Mobilgas, Regent and Esso tankers. This model was finished in blue and dark-blue. A great pity it did not carry any petrol company names on the side. Original Price 9/6

Rarity Value: Easily obtained

Introduced in 1949, Number 40d. Austin A40 Devon, a most attractive model with the typical rounded lines of the period. Finished in greyish green with cream wheel hubs. Original Price 1/9

Introduced in April 1951, Number 140a. The Austin Atlantic Convertible, a very attractive model realistically displaying the large bulbous flowing wings of the real car. Fitted with a fully detailed interior and dash with a separate steering wheel. Finished in black with red interior and white tyres. Original Price 3/4

Rarity Value: Easily obtained

Rarity Value: Rare

Introduced in January 1952, Number 505. The Type I Foden Flat Truck with chains being produced for only eight months has become one the rarest Dinky models. Finished in medium-green with pale-green wheel hubs and cab flash this superb truck is very difficult to obtain; the model shown in the above photograph is one of the few surviving, genuine, examples. In Sepember 1952 the Type 2 Foden Chain Truck replaced the above vehicle and featured a newly designed cab. Original Price 11/6

Introduced in April 1951, Number 29G. The Luxury Coach is finished in fawn with an orange flash and mudguards. Judging by the style of the radiator grille this model may have been influenced by the Maudsley or A.E.C. radiator design. Original Price 3/1

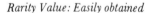

Rarity Value: Easily obtained

Rarity Value: Rare

Introduced in 1952, French Dinky, Number 32-AJ. The Panhard Articulated Truck is quite rare and has qualities not often found in British Dinky models therefore making an interesting model, finished in yellow with red 'Kodak' advertising on the side

Introduced in 1952, French Dinky, Number 24S. The Simca 8 Sport is an exceptional model which managed to capture the lines of the original car very well. This model was finished in pale blue with red interior

Rarity Value: Fairly rare

Rarity Value: Fairly rare

Introduced in September 1952, Number 591. The A.E.C. Monarch Thompson Tank 'Shell Chemicals Ltd' changed in 1954 to 'Shell Chemicals'. Faithfully reproduced by Dinky this model has been finished in red and yellow with the typical A.E.C. cab of that period. Original Price 8/8

Introduced in February 1953, Number 533. The Leyland Comet Portland Cement Truck was a very accurate model, authentically finished in yellow with the company names on the side. Original Price 6/-

Rarity Value: Fairly rare

Rarity Value: Very rare

Introduced in 1953, Number 504. Foden 14-ton Tanker featuring the new design of cab which was a very attractive one. Shown here is the rather rare plain version. Finished in red and fawn

Introduced in 1953, French Dinky, Number 24N. The Citroen 11BL compared with its predecessors features a built-out boot, wider back window and modified bumpers. Finished in light grey this model completes a long line of Citroens

Rarity Value: Fairly rare

Rarity Value: Fairly rare

Introduced in 1954, French Dinky Number 24v. The Buick Roadmaster, one of the best detailed American cars ever produced by Dinky, fitted with white rubber tyres and finished in pale yellow with a dark-green roof

Introduced in 1954, French Dinky, Number 32-C. The Panhard Esso Road Tanker fitted with a catwalk and ladder in tinplate is an attractive model finished in deep red with a white flash also bearing an 'Esso' motif on the sides and rear.

Rarity Value: rare

Rarity Value: Easily obtained

Introduced in April 1955, Number 108. MG TF Midget, the last of the classic MG open 2-seaters as portrayed by Dinky. Competition version shown fitted with a steering wheel pinned into the dashboard, a metal driver in racing overalls and a transparent plastic windscreen. Finished in red with tan interior and racing numbers '24' on the bonnet and doors. Original Price 3/9

Introduced in 1955, Number 107. Sunbeam Alpine shown here in competition form with racing driver and number '26' on the side. Finished in pale blue with cream interior. Original Price 3/11

Rarity Value: Easily obtained

Rarity Value: Easily obtained

Introduced in Febuary 1956, Number 111. Triumph TR2, competition version shown fitted with steering wheel pinned to the dash, racing driver and a transparent plastic windscreen. Finished in pink with blue interior and racing number '29' on bonnet and door. This model was also available as a touring car without racing number. Original Price 3/6

Introduced in July 1956, Number 163. The Bristol 450 Sports Coupe was modeled on the 1954 Bristol Le-Mans car, the body being surprisingly streamlined compared to that of previous Le-Mans models. Finished in green the overall sporting effect is completed by racing numbers on doors and bonnet. Original Price 2/9

Rarity Value: Fairly rare

Rarity Value: Rare

Introduced in December 1933, Set 22, Modeled Miniatures comprising 22a Sports Car price 6d, 22b Sports Coupe price 6d, 22c Motor Truck price 8d, 22d Delivery Van price 8d, 22e Tractor price 9d and 22f Tank price 1/-. Price of complete set 4/-. These were the first offerings from Meccano. The closed coupe is based on the SS1 Jaguar while the tractor could well be based on the Fordson model of that time; the metal they were cast in contained mostly lead which accounts for the fact that they do not suffer from metal fatigue. As a set they are rather a mixed bunch but containing a fine vintage character typical of the 1930s.

Introduced in 1934, 28/1 Series Delivery Vans are shown in this and the following four photographs. Number 28c 'Manchester Guardian', 28a 'Hornby Trains', 28b 'Pickfords Removals,' 28i 'Crawfords Biscuits' and 22d 'Meccano Engineering'

Introduced in May 1934, Number 28m. 'Wakefields Castrol Motor Oil'. The first type-I Van to carry advertising on the sides was Number 22d, 'Meccano Engineering for Boys', finished in the plain 22 series colours. In 1934 it appeared in the 28 series, although carrying a '22' number, finished in yellow as shown in the previous photo

Introduced in 1934, 28/1 Series Delivery Vans. 28f 'Palethorpe's Sausages', 28d 'OXO Beef in Brief', 28i 'Ensign Cameras', 28h 'Sharp's Toffee' and 28g 'Kodak Cameras'

Introduced in September 1934, Number 28e.Delivery Van 'Firestone Tyres'. Photo courtesy Eric Morgan

Introduced in 1934, 28/1 Series Delivery Vans. Number 28n. 'Marsh's Sausages', 28i carrying 'Ensign Lukos Films', on the right-hand side and 'Ensign Cameras' on the left, 28d 'OXO' and No 25d 'Power' Petrol Tanker introduced in 1939, original price 9d. These are the most sought-after, and also the most expensive, models and are very rare. The type-1 vans were manufactured from 1934 to 1935; one or two were fitted with rubber tyres as shown on No 28in. This collection of type-1 Vans is owned by Eric Morgan, one of the few collectors with a full set of type-1 vans in this country, all of which are completely original. Original price 9d each.

Rarity Value (all type 1 Vans): Very rare, (25d Tanker): Very rare

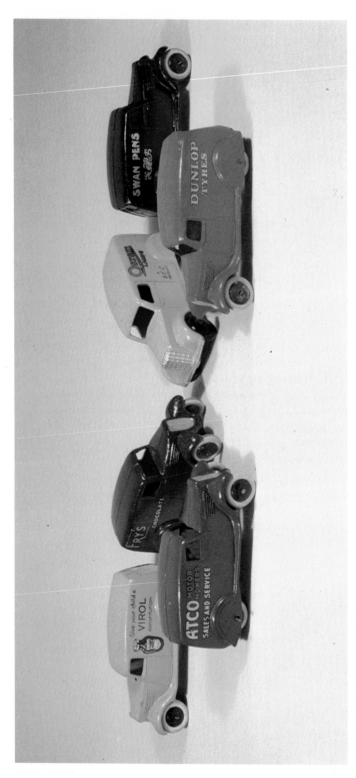

Rarity value (type-2 and -3): Very rare

Introduced 1935, 28/2 Series Delivery Vans. The largest set of small vans produced by Meccano; no less than thirty one were introduced, all of which are very scarce due to the fact that they suffer badly from metal fatigue. Shown in this photograph are 28f 'Virol', 28h 'Dunlop Tyres', 28r 'Swan Pens', 28s 'Fry's', 28n 'Atco' and a 28/3 Series Van, number 28w 'Osram'. The type-2 vans replaced the type-1 already described and were produced from 1935 until 1939 when they were replaced by the type-3 vans as depicted by Number 28w 'Osram' of which there were twelve introduced. This version of type-3 continued after the war as a plain van and a loudspeaker van. The type-3 with advertising was produced only for a short period, therefore they have become very scarce. Original prices were 6d each.

Rarity Value: Rare

Introduced in 1938, Number 29c. Double-Decker Bus (A.E.C.). Shown here are two original pre-War examples with the staircase inside, a feature left out in post-war versions. Original Price 1/-

Introduced in 1953, Number 27n. Field Marshall Tractor. Original price 4/4

Rarity Value: Easily obtained

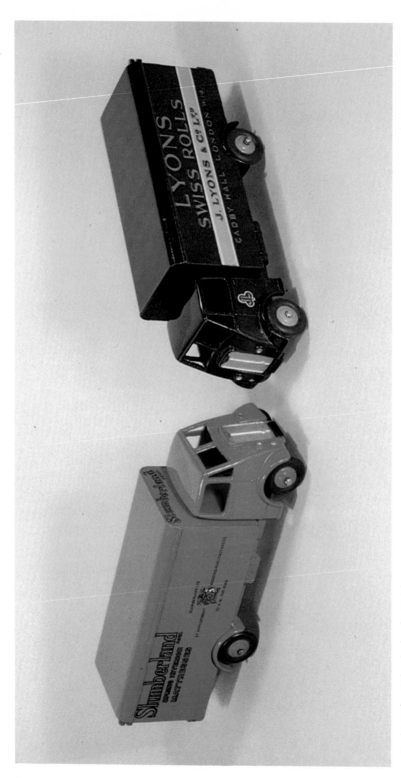

Rarity Value (Slumberland): Fairly rare

(Lyons): Very rare

Introduced in December 1949, Number 514. Guy Van 'Slumberland', original price 5/8. Also shown is No 514 Guy Van 'Lyons Swiss Rolls', introduced in November 1951, this was the second Guy Van to be introduced and one of the smartest. The 'Slumberland' model was the first to be introduced. Original price for the 'Lyons' van was 7/9

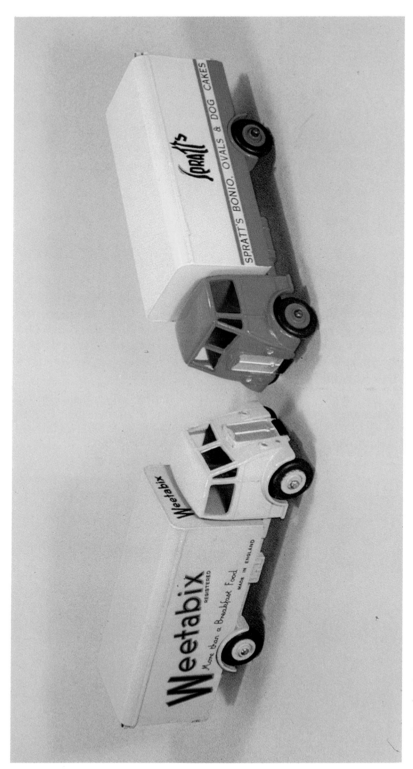

Rarity Value (Spratts): Fairly rare
(Weetabix): Very rare

Introduced in June 1952, Number 514. Guy Van 'Weetabix' one of the rarest of the Guy Vans, original price 7/9. Also shown is No 514 Guy Van 'Spratts' which was the fourth one to appear becoming available in July 1953: original price 7/-

Rarity Value (Ever Ready): Easily obtained
(Golden Shred): Fairly rare

Introduced in December 1955, Number 918. Guy Van 'Ever Ready Batteries', possibly the easiest version of Guy Vans to find; its original price was 8/-. Also shown is No 919 Guy Van 'Golden Shred', introduced in June 1957; this was the last of the Guy Vans to feature the earlier style of cab and one of the best. As with all the Guy Vans the rear doors open. Original price 8/9

Introduced in 1958, Number 923. (*Left*) Big Bedford 'Heinz' with tomato ketchup bottle transfer introduced to replace the previous versions depicting a tin of baked beans. Original price 8/9. (*Right*) Number 920. Guy Warrior 'Heinz' Van introduced in 1959/60 to replace the Big Bedford 'Heinz' Van. Original price 8/9. This model is probably the most expensive and sought after post-War Dinky Toy available.

Rarity Value (920) : Rare
(923): Rare

Rarity Value (Esso): Fairly rare, (Dunlop): Fairly rare, (OXO): Very rare

Introduced in February 1951, Number 31a. Trojan Van 'Esso' this was the first of the six Trojan Vans made by Meccano, original price 2/6. The second version to be introduced was Number 31b Trojan Van 'Dunlop' available June 1952; its original price was 2/11. Also shown is No 31d Trojan Van 'OXO' which was the fourth one to appear being introduced in 1953 and produced for only a few months, making it the rarest of the Trojan Vans. Original price 2/2

Introduced in September 1953, Number 31c Trojan Van 'Chivers Jellies'; this was the third Trojan to be introduced. Original price 2/2. The fifth version was probably the most attractive, namely, Number 454 Trojan Van 'Cydrax' introduced in February 1957. Original price 2/9. The last to be introduced, in May 1957, was Number 455 Trojan Van 'Brooke Bond Tea', a company famous for using Trojan Vans of years gone by; original price 2/9

Rarity Value (Chivers): Fairly rare, (Cydrax) : Fairly rare, (Brooke Bond Tea): Fairly rare

Rarity Value: (Shell-BP): Fairly rare, (Nestle's): Fairly rare, (Raleigh Cycles): Rare

Introduced in May 1954, Number 470. Austin A40 Van 'Shell-BP' based on the famous A40 Devon car. This was the first version available, original price 2/11. The next one was introduced in October 1955, Number 471 Austin A40 Van 'Nestle's; original price 2/9. The last and most attractive was introduced in April 1957, number 472 Austin A40 Van 'Raleigh Cycles', original price 2/9

Introduced in June 1954, Number 480. Bedford Van 'Kodak', the first to be introduced in this set of three, original price 2/9. The next version to appear was number 481 Bedford Van 'Ovaltine', introduced in Setpember 1955, original price 2/9. The last to appear was Number 482 Bedford Van 'Dinky Toys' in Meccano colours of that period, introduced in October 1956, original price 2/9

Rarity Value (Kodak): Rare, (Ovaltine): Fairly rare, (Dinky Toys): Fairly rare

Rarity Value (Royal Mail) : Easily obtained, (Capstan): Very rare, (Telephone Services): Fairly rare

Introduced in May 1955, Number 260. Morris Van 'Royal Mail', a good model, original price 3/-. Shown alongside is Number 465 Morris Van 'Capstan', basically the 'Royal Mail' Van with new and very attractive colours. Introduced March 1957, original price 3/-. The last van shown here is number 261 Morris 8 Series-E, 'Post Office Telephones', one of the best models made by Meccano. Introduced in March 1956, original price 3/3

Introduced in 1953, Number 504. Foden 14-Ton Tanker 'Mobilgas' original price 8/3. Also shown is the handsome Number 942 Foden 14-Ton Tanker 'Regent' available from June 1955, original price 9/6.

Rarity Value (Mobilgas): Fairly rare, (Regent): Fairly rare

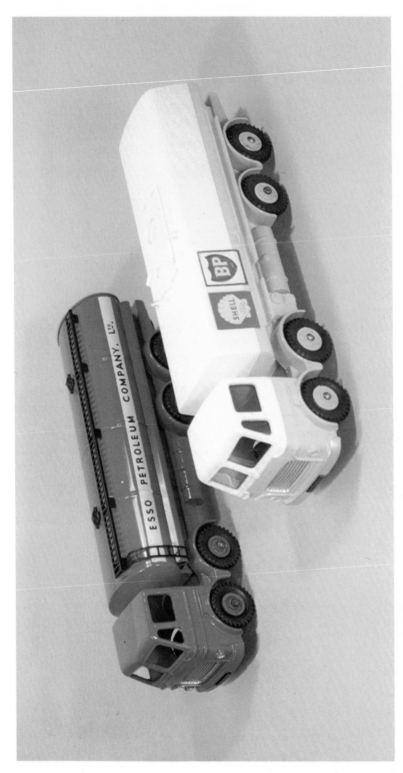

Rarity Value (Esso) : Fairly rare, (Shell-BP) : Fairly rare

Introduced in March 1958, Number 943. Leyland Octopus Tanker 'Esso'; this model carried the same tinplate tank as the earlier Foden, original price 11/6. Shown alongside is the last of the eight-wheeled Tankers, namely, Number 944 Leyland Octopus 'Shell-BP' 4000-gallon Tanker introduced in July 1963. The latter differs from the earlier 'Esso' Tanker in respect of carrying a plastic tank of completely new design, also the cab features fully glazed windows. Original price 11/6.

Rarity Value: Fairly rare

Introduced in May 1957, Number 642. The Leyland Hippo R.A.F. Pressure Re-fueller. Finished in the appropriate R.A.F. blue livery. Original Price 7/9

Introduced in June 1957, Number 661. The Scammell Ten-Ton Recovery Tractor with working jib, finished in the standard olive-drab Army livery. A very nice model and the only Scammell model Dinky ever produced. Original Price 9/6

Rarity Value: Easily obtained

Rarity Value: Rare

Introduced in 1958, Number 431. The Guy Warrior 4-Ton Truck, quite a difficult model to find, finished in pale fawn and dark green, was brought out to replace the previous Guy. It features a completely new chassis and cab containing windows. Original Price 5/9

Introduced in 1958, Number 432. The Guy Warrior Flat Truck, an extremely difficult model to obtain – I have only seen four. Originally brought out to replace the previous Guy range. The same new features have been used as seen in Number 431. The Guy Warriors were the first range of commercials to feature windows. Original Price 6/2

Rarity Value: Rare

Rarity Value: Easily obtained

Introduced in 1958, Number 174. Hudson Hornet fitted with windows; a very well detailed model of one of the last Hudson cars sold in the USA. Finished in yellow and grey. Original Price 3/6

Introduced in November 1958, Number 167. AC Aceca, a very interesting car to model and the only AC produced as a diecast toy. Fitted with transparent windows and finished in cream and brown. Original Price 3/3

Rarity Value: Easily obtained

Rarity value (183): Easily obtained
Rarity value (529): Fairly rare

Introduced in May 1958, Number 183. The Fiat 600. Finished in light green, this car would certainly have looked better with metal wheel hubs and rubber tyres rather than the one-piece plastic wheels. Original Price 2/4. Sharing this photograph the French Dinky Vespa 400 2CV, Number 529 is a compact little model finished in blue with an imitation sunshine roof in grey. This car was introduced in 1959.

Rarity Value: Easily obtained

Introduced in February 1959, Number 150. The Rolls-Royce Silver Wraith, fitted for the first time with spring suspension and plated radiator and bumper. Finished in pale grey and dark gry. Original Price 5/6

Introduced in December 1960, Number 966. The Leyland Comet Marrel Multi Bucket Unit, finished in pale yellow with a grey bucket unit (not to be confused with the earlier Comet cab); this model features a working skip. The skip is operated by pressing the lever on the side which lifts and lowers the bucket unit. Original Price 10/9

Rarity Value: Fairly rare

Rarity Value: Rare

Introduced in April 1961, Number 948. The McLean Articulated Truck clearly displays the firm's interest in the American market making it a very attractive model which is finished in red and grey with opening rear doors. The tractor unit uncouples and the trailer is moulded in plastic with a diecast under-frame and cab. Original Price 16/6

Rarity Value: Rare

Introduced in October 1961, Number 979. The Maudsley Newmarket Racehorse Transporter, finished in pale grey and cream is fitted with hinged side and rear ramps also carrying 'Newmarket' transfers on its side was based on The British Railway horsebox, Number 581 which was finished in deep maroon. Both models are supplied with their own horse. Original Price 15/4

Introduced in 1962, Number 145. Singer Vogue displaying the typical Roots styling which is faithfully reproduced in this model. Fitted with spring suspension and finished in metallic green with red interior.

Rarity Value: Easily obtained

Rarity Value: Rare

Introduced in October 1962, Number 908. The Thornycroft Mighty Antar Tractor and Trailer with transformer is a rare model to find in any Dinky collection. The cab is finished in yellow and the trailer grey with red ramps. Although this model is British the Transformer (named 'ALSTHOM') was actually made in France by Meccano and was originally produced for the French Dinky model Number 898 (Berliet Transformer carrier). Original Price 21/-

Introduced in 1963/64, Number 935. The Leyland Octopus Flat Truck, with chains, was the last of the long line of eight-wheelers to be introduced; again a difficult model to find in good condition. Finished in green and white with red plastic wheel hubs. Original Price 10/9

Rarity Value: Rare

Rarity Value: Fairly rare

Introduced in 1963, Number 291. Leyland Double-Decker 'Exide Batteries'. The final version of the half-cab double-decker produced by Dinky. Finished in red. Original price 4/2

Introduced in September 1964, Number 425. The Bedford TK Coal Truck, finished in red with a silver chassis and fitted with plastic windows and interior, is a detailed model carrying six bags of coal and a set of scales. The lorry also bears the name 'Hall and Co Approved Coal Merchant'

Rarity value: Fairly rare

Rarity Value: Fairly rare

Introduced in 1964, Number 120. Lincoln Continental, a super model with opening bonnet and boot and fully detailed interior. Finished in metallic bronze with a white roof. Original Price 8/11

Introduced in 1964, Number 127. Rolls-Royce Silver Cloud MkIII, with James Young style of coachwork, is fitted with opening bonnet and doors. Finished in deep metallic red. Original Price 9/11

Rarity Value: Fairly rare

Rarity Value: Fairly rare

Introduced in December 1964, Number 275. The Brinks Armoured Car, again showing interest in the American market. An unusual vehicle to model, it was equipped with a driver and guard, doors which open and two crates of gold bars. Finished in white with a navy-blue chassis. Original Price 12/11

Introduced in 1965, Number 402. The Bedford T.K. Coca-Cola Truck. Finished in authentic colours of red and white with the advertisement 'Drink Coca-Cola' displayed on the loading areas, this model also has removable plastic crates and bottles. This truck utilizes the same Bedford T.K. chassis as the T.K. Tipper and Coal Truck. Original Price 9/11

Rarity Value: Fairly rare

Rarity Value: Fairly rare

Introduced in 1965, Number 450. The Bedford TK Castrol Motor Oil Box Van with sliding doors on the side and rear was finished in metallic dark-green with white plastic doors and the company name in red on the sides. Original Price 10/9

Rarity Value: Easily obtained

Introduced in 1965, French Dinky, Number 577. The Berliet G.A.K. Cattle Carrier, finished in light green and yellow, features a ramp which drops down at the rear to allow two cows (supplied) to be loaded

Introduced in 1965, Number 914, A.E.C. Articulated British Road Services Truck featuring a removable canopy and a drop-down tailboard. It uncouples by applying pressure to the dynamo on the tractor unit. The tractor unit is finished in red and the trailer in white; the moulded plastic canopy is green. Original Price 18/11

Rarity Value: Fairly rare

Rarity Value: Fairly rare

Introduced in 1966, Number 156. Saab 96 V4, an excellent model fitted with opening doors, jewelled headlamps and plated grille/bumpers. Finished in metallic red. Original Price 6/11

Introduced in 1966, Number 164. Ford Zodiac Mk IV, one of Dinky's best models featuring jewelled headlamps, tail lights and fully detailed interior. Also all four doors, bonnet and boot can be opened. The model shown here is finished in the rare colour of metallic gold. Original Price 13/11

Rarity Value: Easily obtained

Rarity Value: Easily obtained

Introduced in 1967, Number 945. The A.E.C. Articulated Fuel Tanker 'Esso'. Fitted with rubber tyres this issue was the first to bear the slogan 'Put a Tiger in your Tank'; later versions did not include either of these features. Being a very good model this tanker had a long run in production and was later replaced by the current Foden Burmah Tanker. The Esso Tanker features plastic windows, interior detailing and opening fillers on the tank top and is finished in white with a red flash on the side. Original Price 19/11

Rarity Value: Easily obtained

Introduced in 1967, Number 970. The Bedford T.K. Jones Fleetmaster Cantilever Crane Truck, fitted with windows, seats and a working crane jib which can be swivelled around, raised or lowered. Finished in yellow and black. Original Price 21/6

Introduced in 1968, French Dinky Number 413. The Citroen Dyane, fitted with an opening bonnet and tailgate, also two suitcases were supplied. Finished in white with black interior, this model was produced from 1971 to 1974 in Britain.

Rarity Value: Fairly rare

Rarity Value: Easily Obtained

Introduced in 1968, Number 917. Mercedes-Benz Truck and Trailer, features include: opening doors, detailed interior, door-mirrors, jewelled headlamps, opening cab-roof ventilator, detachable canopies on truck and trailer, opening tailgate, suspension on truck and trailer, and bogie wheels which pivot on the trailer. One of Dinky's best models, also the longest in length. Finished in blue and yellow with white plastic canopies. Original Price 37/11

Introduced in 1969, Number 175. Cadillac Eldorado, a good model of General Motors front-wheel-drive vehicle featuring opening bonnet, doors, boot and fully detailed interior. Finished in metallic purple with a black 'vinyl' roof.

Rarity Value: Easily obtained

Rarity Value: Still Current

Introduced in 1969, Number 285. AEC Merryweather Marquis Fire Tender with operating water pump and extending ladder. Finished in metallic red and silver. Original Price £1 7s 9d

Introduced in 1971, Number 451. The Ford D800 Johnston Road Sweeper, with rotating horizontal and vertical brushes, has swivelling suction pipe and opening cab doors. An excellent model and one which is still current, although the cab doors no longer open. The cab is finished in orange, the tank in metallic green and the chassis in silver. More recently the model has appeared finished in light green all over. Original Price £1.35

Rarity Value: Still current

Rarity Value: Easily obtained

Introduced in 1971, Number 283. A.E.C. Swift Single Decker Bus fitted with a button-operated bell and automatic opening doors. Finished in London Transport red. Original price £1.19

Rarity value: Easily obtained

Introduced in 1973, Number 295. The Atlantian Double-Decker Bus with rear engine, nicely finished in yellow and carrying an advertisement for 'Yellow Pages'. A good clean casting but, unfortunately, fitted with speedwheels which tend to spoil the appearance of the vehicle. Original Price £1.55

Introduced in 1973, Number 924. The Aveling-Barford Centaur Dump Truck, a big sturdy model. By pressing the lever on the side of the cab the spring-loaded tipping action can be activated. This model is finished in red and yellow with a silver chassis. Original Price £3.25

Rarity Value: Still available in some toyshops, although now discontinued

Rarity Value: Easily obtained

Introduced in 1976, Number 604. The Army Land Rover Bomb Disposal Unit. The model has been cleverly covered with a plastic hardtop, based on the old Land Rover Number 344, fitted with opening doors and bonnet and finished in Army matt brown with dayglo orange side panels

Introduced in 1977. The A.E.C. Lucas Oil Tanker was manufactured in limited numbers for Lucas by Dinky as a special sales promotion, therefore this model was not originally intended for retail to the public and therefore does not carry a model number. Finished in the correct livery of green with the company name on the side, this tanker has been based on the A.E.C. Esso Tanker

Rarity Value: Rare

Rarity Value: Still obtainable from some toyshops

Introduced in 1977, Number 297. The Atlantian Double-Decker Bus was produced for 1977 only and finished in silver to commemorate the Queen's Silver Jubilee. Original Price £2.10

Rarity Value: Still current

Introduced in 1978, Number 950. The Foden S20 'Burmah' Articulated Fuel Tanker features opening fillers on the tank top and opening cab doors. Finished in the company livery of red and white. One of the best models to be recently introduced. Current Price £3.99

Introduced in 1978, Number 383. Convoy National Carriers Truck with Dinky's own style cab. It is fitted with a lift off canopy and has speedwheels.This model is constructed mainly from plastic and finished in yellow. A far cry from the earlier models that have been produced in previous years. Price 99p

Rarity Value: Still current

Rarity value: Still current

Introduced in 1978, Number 222. Hesketh 308E Racing Car, a well-finished model featuring fully detailed engine and plated rear suspension. Dark blue, displaying yellow stickers 'OLYMPUS' and number '24.' Current price £1.65

Introduced in 1979, Number 180. The new Rover 3500 is finished in white with black interior. This model features opening doors and tailgate. It is fitted with speedwheels and has a tow-hook on the back. Current price £2.50

Rarity Value: Still current

Rarity Value: Rare

Introduced in 1936, Number 42. Police Hut, Motorcycle Patrol, Point Duty Policeman in white coat, and uniformed Point Duty Policeman. Shown in the original box. Original price of set 1/11

Dinky Supertoys first style of box as shown for Number 501 Foden was introduced in 1947. Plain cardboard was used with a red and white label attached to the top. The other box shown is the second style in which the plain cardboard was covered with blue or green paper and the label attached to the top. This box type was introduced in 1949 and continued until 1954

The first box style introduced for cars and other small vehicles from 1953 was yellow with a colour illustration of the model together with the number and a colour code on the rear. These were produced until 1962. Up until 1953 smaller models, including cars, were not given boxes as they came in dozen packs, for example all Rover 75s. At this time the customer would pick a model in the desired colour and the retailer supplied the paper bag

Introduced in 1955, was the third box style designed for Supertoys. The lid is covered in dark blue stripes with a coloured illustration of the model. Also shown is a variation in which the front of the box is covered by a reproduced colour painting; this style appeared for a short time in the early 1960s

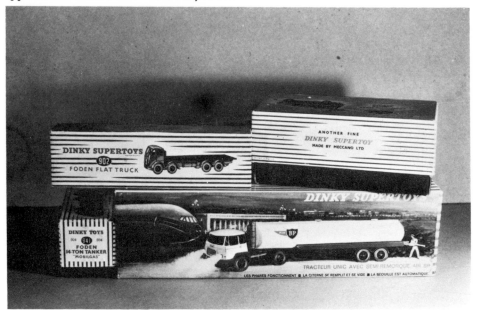

Introduced in 1963 and the fourth box style to be designed. The colour of this particular box is pale yellow in contrast to the dark blue of previous versions. The lid also changed from dark-blue stripes to solid red and yellow with a coloured illustration of the model

The fifth box style design as shown for Number 435 Bedford TK has been produced from one piece of cardboard with flaps at both ends, coloured grey and red with an illustration of the model on the front and back. This design was also used for the cars and other small vehicles from 1963 until the arrival of the clear plastic lid with yellow nylon base in 1965. Also shown is a later version of this box style introduced in 1969 and produced until 1978

The next stage of box design was the first of the clear packs which, unfortunately, were not as strong as previous designs. Introduced in 1970 and produced until 1978

The current design, introduced in 1978, happily, has reverted to a stronger box with a clear transparent front panel displaying the model

Chapter Three

Spot-On

Triang, already famous for its tinplate Minic series of vehicles, Dublo-railways and other children's toys, entered the diecast toy market in 1959, with a line of diecast vehicles called 'Spot-On'. They were slightly larger in scale (1/42,) than Dinky or Corgi (1/43) and each model featured windows, seats, steering wheel and number plates.

Spot-On models were based on everyday vehicles and most appeared in authentic colours similar to the real vehicles they represented, although there were some exceptions to the rule. Each model came in a blue and yellow chequered box with a yellow compass illustrated on the side to indicate the precision of modelling. Later the box design was changed to red, yellow and black with a transparent front panel displaying the vehicle. Earlier models came complete with a colour picture of the real vehicle together with the technical information relating to it.

In 1960 Spot-On introduced some excellent commercial vehicles which, at the time of writing, are probably amongst the most sought-after and most difficult diecast models to find. In 1962 plated plastic headlamps, bumpers and radiator grilles together with operating parts were introduced; about the same time features such as roof racks loaded with luggage appeared.

Spot-On are noted for producing models of unusual and individual cars such as Bristol, Jenson and Armstrong Siddeley – making collecting interesting and varied.

Although Triang marketed Spot-On for less than ten years, they produced a remarkable selection totalling some one hundred and twenty different models. Today Spot-On vehicles, in good condition, are scarce and fetch more than rival Dinky and Corgi models of the same period. The only place one is likely to find a good selection of Spot-On models available today is at swap meetings where you can buy, sell or exchange models. These meetings are held quite often, up and down the country, at Bournemouth, Yeovil, Windsor and Gloucester, to name but a few of the regular venues.

Introduced in 1959, number 101. Armstrong Siddeley Sapphire 236, a well-detailed model displaying the lines of the real vehicle even down to the radiator sphinx mascot. Finished in pale green with a dark metallic-grey roof

Rarity Value: Easily obtained

Rarity Value: Rare

Introduced in 1959, number 103. Rolls-Royce Silver Wraith. The coachwork design closely follows that of James Young with the sweeping wings, roof and boot lines. Finished in silver grey and metallic green

Introduced in 1959, number 104. MGA Sports is a firm favourite with MG fans; this model captures the lines of the original car very well with its familiar MG grille. The model comes complete with fully detailed dashboard. Finished in red with grey interior. Photographed alongside is number 108. Triumph TR3A Sports which was the last of the early series of TR Sports; again a super model featuring the classic sports car line with its cut-down door and protruding headlamps. Finished in pale blue with grey interior.

Rarity Value (104 & 108): Fairly rare

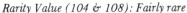

Rear view of No 108 Triumph TR3A Sports, showing the dashboard transfer detail and driving mirror

Introduced in 1959, number 107. Jaguar XKSS, the only diecast model produced of this exciting car of which only seventeen full-size vehicles were produced by Jaguar Cars. Finished in dark green with grey interior and fitted with plastic screen slotted through the body. Also shown is number 105, Austin-Healey 100/6 Introduced in 1959 but was not one of Spot-On's best models. Finished in pale yellow with grey interior.

Rarity Value (107 & 105): Rare

Another view of number 105 Austin Healey 100/6

Introduced in 1959, number 120. Fiat Multipla, a very well-balanced model fitted with spring suspension and finished in pale green.

Rarity Value: Easily obtained

Rarity Value: Fairly rare

Introduced in 1959, number 131. Goggomobil Super; a superb model of this small economy car. Finished in red and black

Introduced in 1959, number 154. Austin A40 was the first of BMC Farina designed models, faithfully copied by Spot-On. This model is fitted with suspension. Finished in pale blue with a black roof

Rarity Value: Fairly rare

Rarity Value: Rare

Introduced in 1960, number 109. E.R.F. Flat Bed, carrying planks of wood. Spot-On trucks are noted for the excellent way in which the chassis detail has been reproduced, particularly the propshaft and back axles. Also the wheels and tyres are very lifelike. Fitted with seats, steering wheel, fully glazed cab and carrying the traditional E.R.F. motif on the radiator. Finished in cream, silver and black.

Introduced in 1960, number 110. A.E.C. Mammoth Major, 'London Brick Company Ltd', carrying the correct load of bricks and finished in red with black cab roof and silver chassis; an excellent model

Rarity Value: Rare

Rarity Value: Rare

Introduced in 1960, number 111. Ford Thames Trader Articulated Truck carrying timber. This model is basically the B.R. Thames Trader but with a load and finished in pale blue

Rarity Value: Rare

Introduced in 1960, number 111. Ford Thames Trader Articulated Truck 'British Railways', one of the best commercials made available. Fitted with the correct coupling gear and finished in the old B.R. colours of maroon and white.

Introduced in 1960, number 112. Jenson 541, a super model of this individual British car, which is fully detailed even down to the sidelamps on top of the wings. Finished in orange

Rarity Value: Fairly rare

Rarity Value: Fairly rare

Introduced in 1960, number 113. Aston Martin DB3. A true classic with its low roofline: the photo shows an early model carrying the first style of wheel hubs. Finished in metallic green with cream interior.

Introduced in 1960, number 118. BMW Isetta Bubble Car, a once familiar sight on the roads. A super little model finished in pale blue.

Rarity Value: Fairly rare

Rarity Value: Fairly rare

Introduced in 1960, number 119. Meadows Friskysport. A very interesting model of this rare car which has been successfully reproduced, finished in green and black

Introduced in 1962, number 137. Massey Harris Tractor. Fitted with authentic steering this is a superb model with fully detailed engine. Finished in red and grey and complete with farmer

Rarity Value: Very rare

Rarity Value: Fairly rare

Introduced in 1962, number 217. Jaguar 'E' Type Fixed Head Coupe. This model features an opening bonnet, suspension, fully detailed interior and plated parts. Again an excellent model capturing fully the lines of the real car. Finished in red with cream interior. Original Price 6/11

Introduced in 1962, number 306. Humber Super Snipe Estate Car. Fitted with roof rack, luggage, driver and passenger. The bodywork displays the typical Humber line of that time; even the wing mirrors are included. Finished in pale blue. Original Price 5/11

Rarity Value: Fairly rare

Rarity Value: Fairly rare

Introduced in 1960, number 110. A.E.C. Mammoth Major 8. Finished in 'British Road Services' livery with the lion over the wheel emblem on the cab

Introduced in 1961, number 110. A.E.C. Mammoth Major 8 'Shell-BP' Tanker. This model features a diecast cab/chassis and plastic tank. This beautifully detailed truck is very much sought after by collectors

Rarity Value: Rare

Rarity Value: Rare

Introduced in 1963, number 110. A.E.C. Mammoth Major 8 'Shell-BP' Tanker, showing the later colours. Produced only for a short time

Introduced in 1963, number 158. Bedford 'S' Type Articulated 'Shell-BP' Tanker, fitted with the correct coupling for the trailer. One of Spot-On's best models

Rarity Value: Rare

Rarity Value: Very rare

Introduced in 1963, number 145. A.E.C. Routemaster Double-Decker Bus. Featuring 'London Transport' livery this is a superb model with fully detailed interior and carrying the appropriate adverts and destinations. The most sought after double decker bus

Introduced in 1964, Set number 806. 'Royal Occasion' featuring a superb model of H.M. the Queen's Rolls-Royce Phantom V Limousine with H.M. the Queen and Prince Philip in the rear compartment. Also supplied are six Guardsmen; a set to be proud of. Original price 25/-

Rarity Value: Rare

Rarity Value: (Bentley): *Very rare,* (Daimler): *Fairly rare,* (MG): *Fairly rare*

Introduced in 1964, number 263. Bentley 4.5-litre. A beautiful model featuring fully detailed dashboard, plated parts and transparent windscreen. Shown in the centre is number 215 Daimler SP250 'Dart' sports car, introduced in 1962. Again an excellent model of an unusual car and the only version of this model with spring suspension and plated parts. Finally, number 279 1936 MG PB Midget introduced in 1965

Rarity Value: Fairly rare

Introduced in 1963, number 117. 'Jones' Crane Truck, one of the best crane trucks ever produced with a working crane jib. Finished in the authentic colours of 'Jones' – red, grey and black

Introduced in 1963, number 155. Austin Taxi. Probably the best model of this classic taxi which is still produced by BL today. Finished in the usual black with cream interior and featuring fully sprung wheels.

Rarity Value: Fairly rare

Rarity Value: Very rare

Introduced in 1963, number 156. Mulliner Luxury Coach based on the Earls Court Show model Guy Warrior. An excellent model of a rather ugly vehicle, finished in pale blue and white with a red flash

Introduced in 1963, number 185. The Fiat 500. This model came complete with plated parts right down to the last detail even the wing mirrors. Fitted with suspension and brightly finished in red with cream interior

Rarity Value: Easily obtained

Rarity Value: Fairly rare

Introduced in 1963, number 191. Sunbeam Alpine. A pleasing model fitted with a plastic hardtop, spring suspension, plated bumper and radiator grille. Finished in pale blue with a black hardtop. Original Price 3/11

Introduced in 1963, number 207. Wadham Ambulance. An extremely good model of this BMC vehicle, fitted with opening rear doors, fully sprung suspension, driver and mate. Finished in cream

Rarity Value: Rare

Rarity Value: Fairly Rare

Introduced in 1963, number 210/2. Morris Mini Van 'Post Office Telephones'. This model is finished in the old P.O. Telephones colour of green with a gold crown transfer on the side. One of the best models of the Mini Van ever produced.

Introduced in 1963, number 211. Austin Seven Mini. This version is an early one. For some reason Minis seem difficult to reproduce in miniature, however, this particular vehicle has been well finished and features spring suspension and plated parts, interior fittings, etc. Finished in pale blue with cream interior. Original Price 3/11

Rarity Value: Fairly rare

Rarity Value: Fairly rare

Introduced in 1963, number 259. Ford Consul Classic with sliding roof. This is a most accurate model, which typifies the styling of Ford's short-lived Consul Classic. Fitted with plated parts and suspension and finished in red with cream interior

Introduced in 1963, number 261. Volvo P1800 fitted with opening bonnet, detailed interior, plastic plated bumpers and radiator grille. Finished in pale blue. Original Price 6/6

Rarity Value: Easily obtained

Rarity Value: Fairly rare

Introduced in 1963, number 193. NSU Prinz. Fitted with spring suspension, plated parts and finished in pale grey.

Introduced in 1964, number 265. Bedford 'Tonibell' Ice Cream Van. Fitted with sliding windows and ice cream attendant who leans out when the van is pressed down on its suspension. Finished in blue with red flash displaying 'Tonibell Dairy Ice Cream' and cow transfers on the sides. Original Price 8/11

Rarity Value: Fairly rare

Rarity Value: Easily obtained

Introduced in 1964, number 267. MG 1100. A delightful model fitted with opening bonnet, the correct MG grille and an anti-mist screen on the rear window. Finished in smoke blue and white. Original Price 5/11

Introduced in 1964 and 1965, numbers 219 Austin Healey Sprite and 281 MG Midget. Showing that even 'badge-engineering' can be scaled-down! Both cars are fitted with the correct radiator grille and badges; each is complete with the same driver. The Austin is finished in pale blue and the MG in red. Original Prices 4/6 and 5/11 respectively.

Rarity Value: Fairly rare

Rarity Value: Fairly rare

Introduced in 1965, number 274. Morris 1100 with canoe. This model features opening bonnet with fully detailed BMC transverse engine and luggage rack with canoe. Finished in pale blue with red interior. Original Price 6/11

Introduced in 1965, number 276. Jaguar 3.4 'S' Type. A beautiful model of a super car with a driver and passenger inside, spring suspension and plated parts. Finished in metallic gold (note the Somerset registration number). Original Price 5/11

Rarity Value: Fairly rare

Rarity Value: Easily obtained

Introduced in 1965, number 278. Mercedes-Benz 230SL. Complete with lady driver and passenger, spring suspension, plated bumper and radiator grille. Finished in metallic red. Original Price 5/11

Introduced in 1965, number 287. Hillman Minx with roof rack and luggage. One of Spot-On's best models fitted with springs and plated parts. Finished in pale green with red interior. Original Price 5/11

Rarity Value: Fairly rare

Rarity Value: Rare

Introduced in 1965, number 289. Morris Minor 1000. One of the most famous cars ever produced. Spot-On have managed to create an excellent reproduction fitted with fingertip steering, springs and plated plastic parts. Finished pale blue with red interior. Original Price 4/11

Introduced in 1965, number 307. Volkswagen Beetle 1200. A very neat model of this famous car. Finished in metallic blue

Rarity Value: Rare

Rarity Value: Rare

Introduced in 1965, number 315. Commer Window Cleaners Van. An excellent model boasting extendable ladders, opening rear doors and two crew members. Finished in pale blue and displaying 'Glass & Holmes Window Cleaning Company' in yellow on the sides

Introduced in 1965, number 410. Austin 1800 with rowing boat. Fitted with an opening bonnet, spring suspension and plated parts. Finished in sandy beige. Original Price 6/11

Rarity Value: Fairly rare

Rarity Value: Rare

Introduced in 1965, Gift Set number 805 'Fire'. Included in this set are a Land Rover and trailer, tommy spot (small boy), two firemen with water hoses and a cardboard building which can be made up. Models finished in the typical red. Original Price 12/6

Introduced in 1965. Lambretta Scooter. Finished in pale blue. The only motorcycle model produced by Spot-on. A very tiny but well-detailed model with pivoting front wheel.

Rarity Value: Rare

Rarity Value: Very rare

Introduced in 1966, number 401. Volkswagen Variant Estate. This model is fitted with an opening bonnet and is rather spoiled by a white plastic tailgate which also opens; otherwise a very good model which is hard to find. Finished in dark blue.

Introduced in 1966, number 402. Land Rover 'Motorways Crash Service' featuring working winch. By turning the plastic wheel the tow hook is lowered or raised. Brightly finished in orange with 'Motorways Crash Service' in blue

Rarity Value: Rare

Rarity Value: Fairly rare

Introduced in 1966, number 450. Land Rover 'R.A.F. Fire Service'. This model is again based on the familiar Land Rover so popular with toy companies. Finished in the traditional R.A.F. blue

At the top of the picture is Spot-on's first box design for cars, introduced in 1959. The lower box was used for big commercials and was introduced in 1960

The second box design for cars, with an illustration of the model on the outside. Also shown is the colour picture of the actual car with the technical data on the back, which was included. These pictures could be filed in a folder

Spot-On presentation pack, containing four sports cars. Introduced in 1961

The last box design featuring a transparent front displaying the model. Introduced in 1965

Spot-On catalogue 1966, price 2d

Chapter Four

Corgi Toys

'Corgi Toys', registered trademark of Playcraft Toys Ltd first appeared in 1956, introducing for the first time transparent plastic windows. I well remember the first issues to appear in toyshops, proudly displaying the slogan 'The ones with the windows' on the front of the boxes which were blue with a coloured illustration of the vehicle. Prices were around 2/-. The cars themselves were based on familiar models of the period. Several of the early models were fitted with a simple push-and-go friction-motor driving the rear wheels.

Light commercials soon followed with the introduction of the familiar Bedford CA Van, which appeared in various forms such as 'AA Automobile Association', 'Corgi Toys' and 'Dunlop'.

In 1959 working suspension was made available with the Chevrolet Impala Police Car and Renault Floride; the suspension worked by means of two tension bars running side by side on the baseplate across the axle clamped behind, and in front of, each wheel: as the model is pressed down the suspension comes into action. In 1960 Corgi excelled themselves with the Aston Martin DB4 GT with opening bonnet – the first time this had been featured on any proprietary diecast model car. Also in 1960 the boxes changed to yellow and blue with a coloured picture of the model on the side. 'Corgi Major Toys' were introduced in 1958; these were Corgi's equivalent of Meccano's 'Dinky Supertoys' although the Corgi range of heavy commercials were somewhat smaller in number being extended more in the 'sixties and 'seventies.

In 1965 the 'James Bond' Aston Martin was made available, quickly making its mark as one of Corgi's best-sellers and still being produced today, although in a slightly larger form. Corgi have produced several models which have a television or film tie-in such as the Beatles' *Yellow Submarine*, *Chitty Chitty Bang Bang*, *Man from U.N.C.L.E.* and *Daktari*. All of these have proved firm favourites with children.

In 1965 Corgi introduced their famous 'Corgi Classics', these being models of vintage and veteran cars which were truly excellent reproductions. The range included the Rolls-Royce Silver Ghost, Bentley 3-litre. Model T Ford, Daimler 38hp and Renault 12/18. Each model featured a fully detailed chassis with separate exhaust system, springs, back axle and engine sump; a driver and passenger were also included.

In 1968 'Golden Jacks' appeared. These were, in effect, four built-in jacks which worked by pulling down the gold lever underneath the model to produce the jacking movement: the wheels could then be removed. To put the wheels back on you simply placed the wheel on the end of the stub axle and pressed the lever back, thus refixing the wheel.

In 1970 'Whizzwheels' were introduced - in effect Corgi's answer to Meccano's 'Speedwheels'. About this time some very good commercial vehicles appeared; for example 'Co-op' Scammell articulated, 'Ferrymasters' Scammell articulated and numerous articulated Mack trucks, all with working features.

In 1975 Corgi moved away from the familiar 1/43 scale and slightly enlarged their models to 1/42. With the changeover some very good models were brought onto the market; they were finished to a very high standard, close attention being paid to detail.

1979 is another interesting year with many new models being released. Looking back through the Corgi history, the Corgi Classics have proved to be the best investment as they are now fetching quite high prices compared to other Corgi models which, generally, do not attract such high prices as Dinky and Spot-On; however this may change as they become more scarce.

Introduced in 1956, number 200. Ford Consul Saloon. One of Corgi's first models which could be bought with, or without, a friction motor. The example shown here is fitted with items from their accessory pack such as number plates and fancy wheel stickers. Finished in cream, brown, green, grey or blue. Original Price 2/9

Rarity Value: Easily obtained

Rarity Value: Easily obtained

Introduced in 1956, number 201. Austin Cambridge Saloon, displaying good detail such as bonnet intake, side lamps and bonnet badge. Definitely one of Corgi's best. Finished in turquoise, grey, light green, orange, cream and metallic green & silver

Introduced in 1956, number 202. Morris Cowley Saloon. The friction-drive version depicted here is a very attractive model and the only post-war Cowley modeled by a toy firm. Finished in blue, grey, green and white & blue.

Rarity Value: Easily obtained

Rarity Value: Easily obtained

Introduced in 1956, number 203. Vauxhall Velox Saloon. This model is actually based on the 1955 full size vehicle which had a smaller back window and shorter chrome flash on the side compared to the 1956 version. A good model displaying all the familiar Vauxhall styling of that time, although for some reason the emblem on top of the bonnet was omitted. Finished in red, yellow and red, cream or orange

Introduced in 1956, number 204. Rover 90 Saloon. The familiar P4 but not one of Corgi's best models. Finished in white, dark green, green or metallic red.

Rarity Value: Easily obtained

Rarity Value: Fairly rare

Introduced in 1956, number 205. Riley Pathfinder; one of the few Riley models produced. This was a fairly accurate model which could be purchased with or without a mechanical push-and-go motor. Finished in red or blue

Introduced in 1958, number 151. Lotus Eleven Le Mans, finished in pale blue. The only proprietary diecast model of this unusual, but beautifully streamlined racing car.

Rarity Value: Fairly rare

Rarity Value: Easily obtained

Introduced in 1959, number 213. Jaguar 2.4-litre Fire Service Car. Finished in red with crest decals on the front door

Introduced in 1960, number 422. Bedford CA 12cwt 'Corgi Toys' Van. This is Corgi's later CA Bedford fitted with one-piece windscreen, mesh grille and ribbed roof. An attractive little model finished in yellow with a blue roof displaying the Corgi motif and lettering

Rarity Value: Fairly rare

Rarity Value: Fairly rare

Introduced in 1961, number 231. Triumph Herald Coupe, fitted with opening bonnet and suspension. Finished in metallic-gold and white

Introduced in 1962, number 233. Heinkel Bubble Car featuring spring suspension and finished in lilac. Original price 3/9

Rarity Value: Easily obtained

Rarity Value: Rare

Introduced in 1962, number 1120. B.M.M.O. Motorway Coach, featuring fully-sprung suspension and finished in the appropriate livery of red and black. A very attractive model fitted with a nicely detailed interior including a toilet cubicle. Original Price 8/7

Introduced in 1963, number 316. NSU Sports Prinz, a neat model fitted with suspension and finished in metallic red.

Rarity Value: Rare

Rarity Value: Fairly rare

Introduced in 1964, Corgi Classic, number 9001. 1927 3-Litre Bentley Le Mans, with erect hood. A finely detailed model which boasts a real copper exhaust system. Finished in red and black. Original price 9/11

Introduced in 1964 Corgi Classic, number 9011. Ford Model T, with folded hood, driver and passenger. A superb model of the 'Tin Lizzie' also featuring fully detailed chassis and rear axle spring. Finished in the classic 'any colour as long as it's black'. Original price 9/11.

Rarity Value: Rare

Rarity Value: Rare

Introduced in 1964 Corgi Classic, number 9013. Ford Model T, with erect hood finished in blue and black. Original price 9/11

Introduced in 1964 Corgi Classic, number 9021. 1910 Daimler 38hp, with driver and three passengers. A super model featuring the traditional fluted Daimler radiator and finished in light red, yellow and black. Original price 10/11

Rarity Value: Rare

Rarity Value: Fairly rare

Introduced in 1965 Corgi Classic, number 9031. 1910 Renault 12/18, featuring the unusual Renault bonnet of that period. An excellent model finished in lavender with black hood. Original price 8/11

Introduced in 1965, number 246. Chrysler Imperial Convertible. Fitted with opening bonnet, boot and doors, driver, passenger and fully detailed interior. Very well finished in dark red

Rarity Value: Fairly rare

Rarity Value: Easily obtained

Introduced in 1965, number 474. Ford Thames 5cwt Martin Walter 'Walls' Ice Cream Van with musical chimes. Fitted with sliding windows, fully detailed ice box, sink and ice cream attendant. By turning the handle at the back the musical chimes play a tune. Finished in light blue and cream

Introduced in 1965, number 485. Austin Mini Countryman with roof rack, surfing figure, surf boards and opening rear doors. An excellent model of the familiar wood-framed Countryman finished in turquoise with brown imitation wood

Rarity Value: Fairly rare

Rarity Value: Fairly rare

Introduced in 1966 Corgi Classic, number 9041. 1912 Rolls-Royce Silver Ghost. The ultimate in miniature Rolls-Royce models with plated parts and fully detailed interior. Finished in silver and black. Original price 13/6

Introduced in 1966, number 491. Ford Cortina MkI Super Estate Car. Featuring imitation wood, plated parts, jewelled headlamps, opening tailgate and suspension. Finished in metallic dark-grey with cream interior. Original price 6/-

Rarity Value: Easily obtained

Rarity Value: Fairly rare

Introduced in 1966 Lotus Gift Set, number 37. Comprising Lotus Elan hardtop, Lotus Elan open sports, Lotus-Climax racing car (not shown), VW Racing Tender, Transporter trailer and spare Elan Chassis. One of Corgi's best gift sets. The Elan chassis can be taken out. Both Elans have bonnets that open to reveal the engine detail. The VW Transporter has a full set of tools on board. The models are finished in: Lotus Elan (open) dark green, (closed) yellow and green, VW and trailer white and red

Introduced in 1967 Corgi Classic, number 9004. 1927 3-Litre Bentley Le Mans with folded hood, finished in green. Original price 9/11

Rarity Value: Fairly rare

Rarity Value: Fairly rare

Introduced in 1967, number 262. Lincoln Continental Executive Limousine. A model full of unusual features such as a battery-operated colour television, fully carpeted interior and boot, opening bonnet, doors and boot. Finished in metallic gold and black. Original price 15/6

Introduced in 1967, number 339. Mini Cooper 'S' Monte Carlo Rally 1967. Fitted with roof rack, spare tyre, fog and spotlamps. Finished in red with white roof

Rarity Value: Easily obtained

Rarity Value: Easily obtained

Introduced in 1967, number 340. Sunbeam Imp Monte Carlo Rally 1967. Finished in metallic blue and white

Introduced in 1967, number 479. Commer VH Minibus with film service camera and cameraman, displaying 'Samuelson Film Service Ltd'. The camera and cameraman can be mounted on the roof or at the rear as shown. An excellent model fitted with suspension and fully detailed interior. Finished in metallic blue and white. Original price 10/11

Rarity Value: Fairly rare

Rarity Value: Easily obtained

Introduced in 1956, number 453. Commer 5-Ton 'Walls Ice Cream' Truck. An excellent model displaying the typical, of this period, Commer cab together with early 'Walls' livery

Introduced in 1958, number 459. E.R.F. 44G 'Moorhouses' Van. Features the wrap-around windscreen and oval radiator grille (with the name 'E.R.F' clearly visible). The van body is the same as that used for the Walls Ice Cream van

Rarity Value: Easily obtained

Rarity Value: Fairly rare

Introduced in 1961, number 1126. Ecurie Ecosse Racing Car Transporter. The famous Jaguar Cars transporter used for carrying the works 'D' Type Jaguars; an excellent model featuring sliding door, drop-down ramp, steering and suspension. The car illustrated is not part of the set

Rarity Value: Fairly rare

Introduced in 1971, number 1100. Mack 'Trans-Continental' Articulated Box Van with sliding doors, opening bonnet, detailed uncoupling gear and fully sprung wheels on tractor and trailer

Introduced in 1971, number 281. Rover 2000TC Series II, with the later styling changes including matt black grille, chrome strips on the sides, bonnet scoops and chin completing a very well-detailed model

Rarity Value: Rare

Rarity Value: Fairly rare

Introduced in 1977, number 471. London Transport A.E.C. Routemaster. Produced specially to celebrate H.M. the Queen's Silver Jubilee and available only during 1977. This model is therefore very sought-after. Original price £1.65

Introduced in 1979, number 1109. Ford 'Michelin' Tilt-Cab Articulated Truck. Featuring detachable tractor unit and a fully detailed engine revealed by tilting the cab; one of the best models introduced in 1979 Current price £4.89

Rarity Value: Current model

Rarity Value: Fairly rare

Introduced in 1969, number 302. Hillman Hunter, London to Sydney Marathon Winner fitted with golden jacks, spot lights, spare wheels, full tool kit mounted on the roof and fully detailed interior. An excellent model of this famous car. Finished in blue and white

Shown together are number 327 MGB GT introduced in 1967 and number 345 MGC GT introduced in 1969. Shown clearly is the difference in bonnet detail; both have opening doors and tailgate together with tilt-forward seats and suitcases. The MGB GT is finished in red while the MGC GT is in the competition colours of yellow and black

Rarity Value: (MGB GT): Easily obtainable, (MGC GT): Fairly rare

number 345, MGC GT showing opening doors

Introduced in 1970, number 301, Iso Grifo 7-Litre, with opening bonnet, doors and tip-forward seats completing a very well-finished model of a super Italian high-performance car. Finished in metallic blue and black

Rarity Value: Easily obtained

Rarity Value: Easily obtainable

Introduced in 1970, number 376. Chevrolet Corvette Stingray. A really superb model with every detail faithfully reproduced; fitted with opening bonnet, pop-up headlamps, built-in jacks and removable roof panels. Finished in metallic green with black bonnet

Introduced in 1970, number 382. Porsche Targa 9IIS. Featuring opening doors, tilt-forward seats, engine compartment lid, fully detailed engine and jewelled headlamps. Finished in metallic green with red interior

Rarity Value: Easily obtained

Rarity Value: Fairly rare

Introduced in 1971, number 306. Morris Marina 1.8 Coupe, fitted with opening doors and Whizzwheels. Finished in metallic red

Introduced in 1971, number 312. Marcos Mantis, fitted with opening doors. A superb model of this very rare car. Finished in metallic dark red

Rarity Value: Fairly rare

Rarity Value: Easily obtained

Introduced in 1973, number 154. John Player Special Lotus racing car, featuring fully detailed engine and suspension. Finished in the classic black and gold associated with this Grand Prix car

The first box design produced from 1956-1958. The box was coloured blue with a colour illustration of the model on two side panels

Shown here are the second and third box designs produced from 1959-1969. The lower box was introduced in 1958 for the Corgi Major Toys series

The current box design, introduced in 1970

Chapter Five

Lesney 'Matchbox' Models of Yesteryear

Lesney, already famous for thier 'Matchbox' series of diecast models introduced a new line in 1956 known as 'Models of Yesteryear'. Their first offerings in the new series were rather a mixed bunch, comprising traction engines, a horse-drawn bus, a steam-locomotive, etc. The casting of these models, which were made entirely of metal, was very fine and well detailed. Yesteryear first issues were produced in a smaller scale than those now current. The boxes have also changed – I remember the first ones very well; they looked very much like a matchbox, being coloured yellow with brown sides and carrying a line drawing of the model on the top panel and the vehicle's history on the back panel.

In 1960, with the introduction of the Rolls-Royce Silver Ghost, seats moulded in plastic were introduced. Most of the models of recent times have tended to be cars although a few commercial vehicles have been recently introduced.

Boxes have changed gradually from the 'Matchbox' image into more elaborate affairs with a transparent front panel displaying the model and a technical description on the back of the box.

Recently the Yesteryear range has been diversified with the introduction of one of the best models yet, the Talbot Van with 'Liptons Tea' markings or 'Chocolat Menier' (for the French market) advertising on the sides. Incidentally, the Talbot Van has proved to be difficult to obtain at the time of writing. Just released is a Ford Model T van with 'Colmans Mustard' or 'Coca-Cola' (for the American market) markings.

Yesteryear models have always been good value for money, allowing both children and adults to make up a collection without spending too much money. Earlier Yesteryear models are very popular amongst collectors, especially the very first series.

Rarity Value: Easily obtained

Introduced in 1960, Number Y15 1st issue. Rolls-Royce Silver Ghost. One of Lesney's best; a well-detailed model even displaying the rivets along the bonnet sides, toolboxes on the running boards, outside spare wheel and the classic Rolls radiator. Finished in pale-metallic green with black seats and grey tyres.

Introduced in 1961, Number Y16. 1904 Spyker, displaying the typical cylinder shape of bonnet, radiator and a single headlamp mounted in the centre, Finished in pale yellow with dark green seats

Rarity Value: Easily obtained

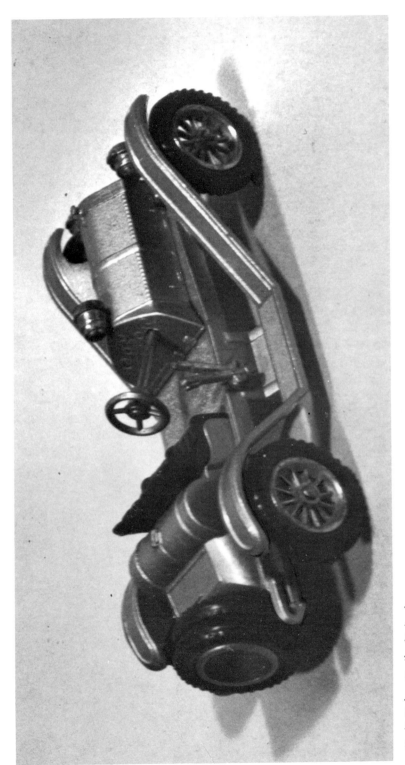

Rarity Value: Easily obtained

Introduced in 1962, Number Y7. 1913 Mercer Raceabout. A delightful model of this famous American car. Lesney have managed to faithfully reproduce the lines of the original car very well with its low build, round fuel tank at the rear, twin spare wheels, outside gearlever and handbrake assembly. Finished in pale metallic lilac with black seats and gold-plated lamps, radiator shell and spoked wheels

Rarity Value: Easily obtained

Introduced in 1964, Number Y11. 1912 Packard Landaulet, featuring outside gearlever, handbrake and gold-plated lamps and radiator shell. Finished in red with black bonnet and black seats with a shield decal on the doors

Rarity Value: Easily obtained

Introduced in 1968, Number Y6. 1913 Cadillac. A very finely detailed model featuring rear-mounted spare wheel, fully detailed hood and gold-plated windscreen, sidelamps, headlamps, radiator shell and spoked wheels. Finished in metallic green with orange seats and black hood

Introduced in 1969, Number Y5, 1907 Peugeot, featuring outside spare wheel and gold-plated windscreen, radiator shell and lamps. A superb model finished in yellow with black roof, red seats and red radiator insert

Rarity Value: Easily obtained

Rarity Value: Easily obtained

Introduced in 1970, Number Y8. 1914 Stutz, featuring gold-plated windscreen, radiator shell and headlamps. Finished in metallic red with green seats and black hood

Introduced in 1973, Number Y11. 1938 Lagonda Drophead Coupe. A fine model featuring fully detailed interior with luggage trunk fitted at the rear and twin side-mounted spare wheels, plus gold-plated radiator shell, bumpers, headlamps and vee-screen. Finished in metallic gold (body), deep purple (mudguards) and black (interior)

Rarity Value: Still current

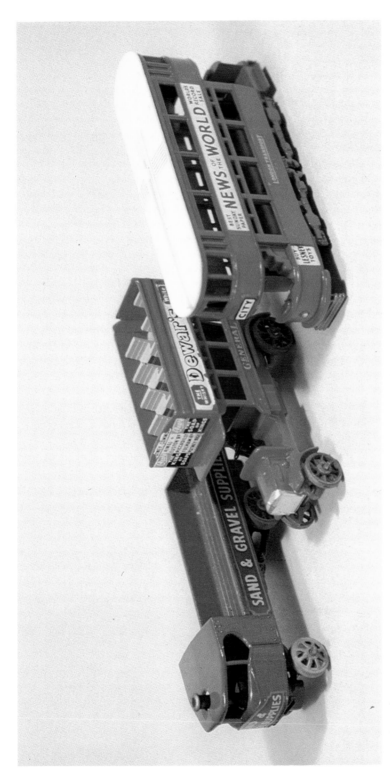

Rarity Value (Y4, Y2 & Y3): Fairly rare

Introduced in 1956, Number Y4. Sentinel 'Sand & Gravel' Steam Wagon. An excellent model displaying the typical open front cab with the chimney passing through the cab roof and chain-driven rear wheels. Alongside is Number Y2 the famous 'Old Bill' B Type Bus. Introduced in 1956 this is a superb model with the typical advertisements on the side (at this time the company was known as 'General' later becoming 'London Transport'). The third model is Number Y3, 1907 London E Class Tram Car, introduced in 1956. An excellent model, carrying the later 'London Transport' name on the sides

Rarity Value (Y9, Y1, & Y11): Fairly rare

Introduced in 1958, number Y9. Fowler Showmans Engine. Surely the best Yesteryear model ever produced, carrying its chimney extension on the roof and with many brass details, so typical of fairground sights of the past. Also shown are Numbers Y1 Allchin 7N H.P. Traction Engine, introduced in 1956, and Y11 Aveling & Porter Steam Roller, introduced in 1958.

Introduced in 1957, Number Y7. 'W & R Jacob & Co', 4-Ton Leyland Lorry displaying superb decals on the sides, also the round side windows and open front cab so typical of the period. Alongside is Number Y6 'Osram Lamps' A.E.C. Y Type Lorry introduced in 1957/58 and displaying the rare colour of dark grey instead of the standard grey

Rarity Value: (Y7): Fairly rare, (Y6): Rare in dark grey, fairly rare in light grey

Rarity Value (Y12 & Y4): Fairly rare

Introduced in 1958, Number Y12. London Horse-Drawn Bus displaying a very high standard of detail. Alongside is Number Y4 Shand Mason Horse-Drawn Fire Engine, introduced in 1961. The version displayed here is the first issue which featured 'Kent Fire Brigade' on the sides. Later versions carried 'London Fire Brigade' on the sides and had black horses instead of white ones

Introduced in 1963, Number Y8. 1914 Sunbeam Motor Cycle with Milford Sidecar. A model full of character but spoilt by the plated finish

Rarity Value: Fairly rare

Rarity Value: Still current, although now in new colours.

Introduced in 1973, Number Y16. 1928 Mercedes SS. One of Lesney's best cars, displaying the long bonnet, twin side-mounted spare wheels and trunk. The model shown here features a green hood instead of the standard black hood making it very rare

Introduced in 1978, Number Y5. 1927 'Lipton's Tea' Talbot Van. By far the best Yesteryear model of recent introduction, it features sidemounted spare wheel and opening rear doors.

Rarity Value: Still current, but now has 'By appointment' coat of arms deleted

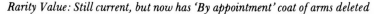

Rarity Value: Still current

Introduced in 1973, Number Y17. 1938 Hispano Suiza. A beautiful model of this all-time classic, featuring detailed dashboard, plated parts and removable hood. Finished in metallic red with black mudguards and black hood

Introduced in 1976, Number Y1. 1936 Jaguar SS100. The forerunner of today's sporting Jaguars and one of the most handsome cars of the 1930s portrayed by Lesney very well. This model features fold-flat windscreen, P100 headlamps, plated radiator, fully detailed interior and spare wheel mounted on the petrol tank. Finished in white with black interior

Rarity Value: Still current

Rarity Value: (R.A.F. Crossley): Still available, (Crossley Coal Truck): Current model

Introduced in 1973, Number Y13, 'R.A.F.' Crossley Tender featuring removable canopy, plated parts and plastic hood. Finished in R.A.F. blue with tan hood and canopy and white seats. Alongside is Number Y13 Crossley 'Coal & Coke' Truck, introduced in 1979 to replace the R.A.F. version. A most attractive model fully loaded with bags of coal, coke and scales. Finished in red and black and displaying 'Evans Bros Coal & Coke' on the sides

Rarity Value (both models): Current

Introduced in 1979, Number Y12/4. Ford Model T 'Colman's Mustard' Van, finished in yellow with black roof, red lining and displaying the bull's head in black with 'Colman's' in red and 'Mustard' in black. Introduced in 1979, No Y12/3. 1912 Ford Model T 'Coca-Cola' Van (for USA market). This model is finished in white with red lining and displays 'Enjoy Coca-Cola' in red

Introduced in 1979, Number Y18, 1937 Cord Supercharged 812. A super model of this highly-prized classic front-wheel-drive car, featuring a plated outside exhaust, bumpers, windscreen, wheels and the famous retracting headlamps. Finished in red with white interior and hood and white wall tyres

Rarity Value: Current

Two examples of Lesney's box design. The one shown at the top is the latest type introduced in 1979. The lower boxes are of the same design (showing the front & back panels) but in different sizes.

Introduced in 1978, two Talbot Vans shown here in their original boxes as produced by Lesney. 'Liptons Tea' (number Y5/3), sold in this country and 'Chocolat Menier' (number Y5/4), which is exported to France.

Rarity value: Current but can be fairly difficult to obtain